Stardust

Poorani Balasundaram

Presentation by *BookLeaf Publishing*

Web: www.bookleafpub.com

E-mail: info@bookleafpub.com

ISBN: 978-93-5744-944-1

First edition 2022

DEDICATION

To all the people who have made me:

Appa and Amma,

Murali Annae,

Arvind Annae,

my vast extended family,

and Poornam Appatha.

To the loves of my life,

Kana, my kutti rowdy,

Groot, my ever-smiling sunshine,

and finally, Dhinu, my Stardust.

ACKNOWLEDGEMENT

I could not have written this book without the love and support of the many people in my life: 'Every action, every word, every step leaves an imprint on this world and the lives of the people around you. Leave only imprints that you would want your children to find.'

This was the most valuable lesson that my parents, Bala and Viji, taught me. And I would not be here if not for the kindness, humility and compassion of these two wonderful human beings.

My husband and partner in crime, Dhinesh (although he likes going by Dhinu), who said to me, "I don't know who was here before, but I am here now," in words and with every action since. Everyone knows you're the better poet. Thanks for being my muse, my rock and my reason.

My beautiful Kana. I have no words to describe the love I have for you. Every minute I lived before you feels like a blur. Thank you for showing me what love is and that love can only grow.

My brothers, Murali and Arvind, who believed in me before I believed in myself. They taught me to be unapologetically persistent and to do what I love.

Poornam Appatha, whose love and life transcends time. The magic of storytelling that you inspired lives in all of us.

Varsha, for being my best critic and inspiration.

BookLeaf Publishing, for making this dream come true.

Last but not least, to the readers. Without you, this book would've been another scribble on an envelope hidden in a closet.

Fallen Gods

The lights in the sky
are shimmering gold,
And the gods have fallen
leaving us so cold.

The nights have passed
and so have you,
Passing clouds, they say
fond memories in whispers blew.

Where do I go
when every road is bare,
And none of them lead to you
neither here nor there.

Stagnant, I suppose,
Still as a stone,
At least I'm here
Albeit all on my own.

The child

They say a child changes everything.

And then you came
and changed the definition of everything.

Just you

I want you
Just you
Raw, untouched, sweet, innocent you.

I want to be with you
in a place
where there's only two
and no one new.

Where we can be
Just be
Unapologetically us
Just us, repercussion-less.

The world will say
what they will say
But you and me
Oh, how much we can be.

Just close your eyes
And feel my hands
Come with me
And take a chance.

So yes – I want you

Just you
Raw, untouched, sweet, innocent you.

I've got you

When the sun goes down
And the ocean sighs,
When the storms collide
And the music dies.

Close your eyes
And hear me sing,
Hear me sing
Your favourite song.

When it feels like war
And every breath is bound,
When you're too far gone
And home is nowhere to be found.

Follow my voice,
Feel my touch,
Take my warmth,
Don't say much.

You're safe – forget not
For I will shelter you,
From monsters and dragons
Grey, white or blue.

I will protect you
Till my last breath and beyond,
I've got you, little one
Inside me you have dawned.

Exist

Today, all I did was exist. That's all I did. I took
a deep breath and forgot about leaving an
impression on the world. I forgot about the
crying child and the aching arms, the sleepless
nights and the mindless fights.
I relaxed my ankles until my feet were floating. I
sank my shoulders and felt the weight lifting. I
sat down on the floor and listened to the beat of
my heart and my blood rushing.

Everything else can wait – the unfolded laundry,
the messy house, the unwashed dishes.
Everything else can wait because everything else
is too hard. Breathing is too hard.

Today, all I did was exist.

Not lovers

Their palms pressed together,
The world fading into an abyss,
Where they're aimlessly floating,
Between the stars and a kiss.

Except he doesn't belong to her,
Nor she to him,
And he will soon be gone,
When this light will forever dim.

This is not love,
But they love each other so,
Perhaps in another lifetime,
there will be more.

Life and Death –
Lovers in the Night

Sitting on the rings of Saturn, he awaits
For the One he loves, her arrival he anticipates.

She arrives, a jar in her hands,
Sorrow in her eyes he never understands.

He brushes off the cosmic dust on his right,
Lays there an old paper before she could fight.

She takes a gulp of air as if it would be her last,
Holding back the tears she sits, thinking of her
past.

She:
I have killed another,
she shouldn't have died,
Oh why, oh why, tell me Life,
Why am I so rotten inside?

He:
You are not rotten, my love,
you are what you're meant to be,

You are the Angel of Death,
It's your job, can't you see?

She:
I am ugly and I am repelling,
I fester like a disease,
I destroy everything I touch,
Anything beautiful, I'll bring it to its knees.

He sighs at his failure, crouching by her feet,
He pinches her chin and feels his skin withering
complete.

She flinches away in shock, gulping the scream
that never came,
the smell of rotting flesh, his beautiful face
melting, oh what a shame.

He:
You burned me because you're hot,
And you're smart and you're kind,
and above all, I love you so
for your beautiful mind.

She:
Are you mad?
We are as opposite as keys and locks,
You are Life and I am Death,
Love between us is a paradox!

He:
Oh sweetheart, so you think,
But we are the same don't you see,
What matters is the perspective,
Think about it with me.

I give life and spread joy,
They think I'm all good,
But I also prolong suffering,
Kill evil, I would if I could.

But you, you let people die,
In peace and with dignity,
You, my beautiful dark angel
You end pain and misery.

She:
Believe me when I say,
I will kill you for I am Death.
And if I do, the giver of life,
That will be the end of every breath.

Tears glimmering in the shining light, she lets
her head fall,
Whatever he said or did, he would never break
her surrounding wall.

And so, she went into the void, nowhere to be found,
Years and aeons passed without a fleeting sound.

And so it goes…

Even though Life and Death have been in love forever,
They can never be together, not now, not ever.

Tu me manques

I miss the changing colours
and the crunching autumn leaves,
The lazy Sunday evenings
acting like dessert thieves.

I miss the midnight food runs
and our movie marathons,
Pretending to be rock stars
singing through the dawns.

I miss camping in the house
And shopping for used furniture,
Leaving random love notes
Every sweet look and every romantic gesture.

I miss the stolen kisses
And the loudest goodbyes
But above all I miss you,
my angel from the skies.

Unmeant

Once spilt forever gone
Words unmeant
Can never be withdrawn.

When you say, "I didn't mean it", I respond, "No one ever does".

In Slumber

Curved eyelashes
Miles long,
Pouty mouth sucking,
To me, you belong.

Your eyes flutter
And fingers dance
Are you playing the piano?
I watch in a trance.

I wish I was there
In whatever your dream may be,
Following you on your adventure,
Charming hero or handsome pirate are ye?

But I'll leave you be
Slumbering under the shining moon,
Sleep now, my little Kana,
For I will see you soon.

You

I will never say this out loud,
but I miss you.

Perhaps it is because when I close my eyes
I can't picture you anymore.

But how could I not?
I've known you all my life.

And yet these memories,
they're mere flashes now.

Now and then I catch a glimpse of a face
like it is on a moving train.

And when they speak your name
The ghost of you lingers like a bloody stain.

My anger has dulled,
But gone I wouldn't say.

And still in your absence
I miss you every day.

I miss you in the core of my bones
and the quietest corners of my mind.

In the longest lines of my palm
and in the smallest veins you'll ever find.

In the faintest breath I have left
and the deepest brown of his eyes.

In the sharpest edges of my soul
and in my loneliest goodbyes.

My Happy Place

I hold you in this quiet, esoteric place
that I keep hidden from another's rein,
Tucked safely in the curve of my smile,
And the endless folds of my fevered brain.

You're my soft ocean breeze
rippling through my hair,
Whispering in my ears,
My answer to every prayer.

You're my handsome ladybug
dotting the young blades of grass,
Fluttering your red velvet wings,
Forever mine howbeit the times that pass.

You're the smell of fresh ground coffee
as I awaken on a lazy Sunday noon,
When the world feels epochs ago,
And you're the bigger spoon.

When your touches set my body ablaze,
When your warmth surrounds me whole,
When your voice feeds my famished mind,
And your kisses breathe life into my gasping
soul.

Appatha... Absolutely

She was brave and she was kind
to everyone and they didn't mind,
Absolute love, she always showed,
With her, no man was left behind.

The lives she touched
they will never forget,
She was in absolute surrender
To every person she met.

She was hurt more than once
by those she loved like daughters and sons,
But her loyalty was absolute
And her time she spent on those ones.

I only wish her life could have seen
The absolute that she had been,
Free to be whoever she wanted
Allowed to be her own queen.

Never someone to hold her tight,
To whisper she was enough with all their might
To tell her that she mattered,
That she was nothing but perfect in their sight.

Whatever it may be
Now she is free
I want her to know that
she'll always be that someone to me.

Stranger

You feel like a distant dream
When I was floating through the cosmos
And you were there with me.

And now I'm in reality
But you feel more like a stranger
than anyone could ever be.

My oldest children

If all I have is today with you
And tomorrow never comes,
I want you to know
That you made me forever young.

With you I was always a child
You cared for me so deep,
You bathed and clothed me
You were the light even in my sleep.

I will forever be grateful
For the life you have given me,
Love, wisdom and kindness
The daughter of your dreams I shall be.

And I do despair
When I have you no more,
What would I do,
My existence shaken to its core.

But in the kindness of his eyes
And the softness of his voice,
I will always find you.
And in your presence, I will rejoice.

3am musings

23

Conflict – suddenly it feels like me against the world.
Only, you're my world.

My little ball of sunshine

Laying under a sycamore tree
You climb over my pregnant belly,
Your incessant sniffing and smiling
Making my body jiggle like jelly.

I try to hold on tight
But you quickly slip away,
And my heart breaks from the loss
Even though I know it's just play.

I watch your golden hair flow
The autumn sun making it shine,
You are all that I truly have
All I have that I can fully call mine.

So all I ask is this,
Slow down a little
And don't grow up so fast,
So I can hold you a little longer
Before you become a whole lot stronger.

Quiet

Why are you so quiet? Why are you so shy?

The endless questions are exhausting just like an extrovert's high.

So, what if she's quiet? What if she keeps to herself?

Sometimes the quietest kinds have the loudest minds.

In utero

I open my eyes and see the silhouette of a child, his wings spread out and flapping in utter joy. I get close and watch mesmerised as a little finger rubs the dirt off his nose, tummy rumbling in a cackle of laughter. He reveals four pearly teeth and nothing more and I haven't seen anything as beautiful before. And right then, I know:

With every little step he takes,
We will grow together,
Floating through life like a feather.

And his big hugs will mend
the little cracks in my soul,
piece by piece until I am whole.

Moments from now, when I open my eyes, he won't be there. But soon, he'll be here and I will love him with all my heart, I swear.

Shooting Star

There is a mason jar
I keep hidden in my closet,
And every night
I fill it with a shooting star.
When darkness befalls
And you're afraid of the unknown,
I will send up little fireworks
So you can find your way home.

You'll know

The day I say,

'I don't hear the voices in my head, or the music
in my ears,
I can't say the words on my lips or paint the
lines beneath my fingers."

'I can't see the colour of a rainbow or smell my
baby's scent that lingers,
I can't taste the spice of Amma's curries, or use
the damn blinkers.'

You'll know.
You'll know that I am me no more.
And that there's a violence in living so sore.

When you do,
Take my hand in yours
Kiss me real slow
And please sweetheart, let me go.

9 789357 449441